the wit
and
wisdom
of wealth
and
philanthropy

Randy Fox, Project Director
Jeff Scoggins, Editor

Library of Congress Cataloging-in-Publication Data
Philanthropic Service for Institutions, 1996
Accent on Humor III: Philanthropy Illustrated
Includes bibliographic references.
ISBN 0-9643585-1-4
Library of Congress Catalog Card Number: 96-71190

philanthropy illustrated

Contents

philanthropy illustrated
Foreword

H umor is the ingredient that makes life's mixture the most palatable. It's like dessert. Washington Irving said "Honest, good humor is the oil and wine of a merry meeting, and there is no jovial companionship equal to that where the jokes are small and the laughter abundant." Since philanthropy is one of the most serious responsibilities we have, why not sprinkle it, along with our conversations and presentations, with some humor.

One of the most effective ways you can use this book is to give it to key donors and volunteers. But don't just send it with your best wishes. Select an appropriate cartoon that reminds you of your colleague. Write a dedicatory note to that person inside the cover referencing the cartoon which "reminds me so much of you and your indefatigable efforts in behalf of this institution." Try it, you'll find it a good time investment.

Philanthropic Services published the first edition of *Accent on Humor* in 1988. It was so popular that a second volume was compiled in 1992. Thousands of volunteers, trustees, administrators, and staff have expressed appreciation for these two editions because the humor helped sparkle their philanthropic endeavors.

Their enthusiastic interest and support of humor in philanthropy prompted this third volume.

This new edition of *Accent on Humor* is dedicated to those men and women who exemplify the spirit of giving that makes the United States the world's central bank for compassion and disinterested love.

Philanthropy has been and will always be a matter that seeks thoughtful and sober reflection. But because people are the principals involved, moments of stress and concern are many. The most effective cure: humor and lightheartedness. So consider *Accent on Humor* a prescription (the chocolate kind) to help you find the lighter side, and maybe even make you laugh at yourself.

Nothing is more serious or important in life than caring and showing love for family, friends, colleagues, and the destitute. But serious and important doesn't mean dark or sad. Make wit, laughter, and light moments a part of the process. You and your work for philanthropy will be better off.

Philanthropic Service for Institutions at the Adventist World Headquarters is pleased to bring this volume to America's philanthropic world as a very modest contribution to the whole. Enjoy your dessert.

Milton Murray
Director Emeritus, PSI

philanthropy illustrated
Introduction

BEETLE BAILEY

BY MORT WALKER

Reprinted with special permission of King Features Syndicate.

philanthropy illustrated
Alumni

"WELL, WE HAD A RATHER ENLIVENED
DISCUSSION AT THE ALUMNI MEETING
TONIGHT"

7
Alumni

"Could you be more specific about the college's financial-aid plan than just, 'What's the current status of your life savings?'"

"I just can't shake the alumni newsletter."

Drawing by Gahan Wilson; © 1987 The New Yorker Magazine, Inc.

Drawing by W. Miller; © 1986 The New Yorker Magazine, Inc.

"...P.S. We are counting on you for a BIG contribution to the Alumni Fund this year."

"HI, I'M FROM YOUR ALUMNI ASSOCIATION."

Harley L. Schwadron

"HERE'S A SWITCH... MY UNIVERSITY ALUMNI ASSOCIATION IS DECLARING A DIVIDEND!"

philanthropy illustrated
Benefactors

"I'm a Supporter. You're a Supporter. Elise, together we could be a Benefactor."

Carole Cable

Mark Litzler

Carole Cable

Benefactors

philanthropy illustrated
Boards

" THE BOARD IS MADE UP OF THREE CONSERVATIVES AND THREE LIBERALS "

"All those in favor of striking the word 'insipid' before 'Board of Directors,' say Aye..."

Contributions Magazine

"Agreed. Board members donating $1 million or more are excused from taking minutes."

Carole Cable

BRING ME YOUR TIRED, YOUR CONFUSED,
YOUR BOARD MEMBERS YEARNING TO GOVERN WELL.

Artist could not be located.

"Apropos of our concern for the environment, we'll recycle all board members for another term."

Carole Cable

"GEE THAT WAS QUITE A COMPUTER VIRUS THAT STRUCK OUR BYLAWS... NOW BOARD MEMBERS ARE REQUIRED TO MAKE A DONATION."

Mark Litzler

"Next year the foundation will focus on grants to teach board members how to raise money."

Carole Cable

philanthropy illustrated
Budgets

" NOW HERE'S A GRAPH THAT GOES UP, FOR A CHANGE. IT'S OUR CASH OUTFLOW "

Copyright, Grantland Enterprises, Inc.; 460 Bloomfield Ave., Montclair, NJ 07042

"By the way, our office space is at a premium right now, so we've made temporary accommodations for you."

philanthropy illustrated
Charity

LITZLER

"CHARITABLE GIVING ISN'T THE ULTIMATE TEST OF ONE'S HUMANITY BUT IT GIVES US SOME NUMBERS TO PLAY WITH."

Mark Litzler

by Brant parker and Johnny hart

DAVE CARPENTER...

"PERHAPS HE WAS DISPICABLE AND UNCARING, BUT IT
WAS HIS WISH TO LEAVE IT ALL TO CHARITY..."

HAGAR THE HORRIBLE

"HEY DAD, HAVE YOU EVER HEARD THAT CHARITY BEGINS AT HOME?"

Joseph A. Brown

"If it's going to charity, then I want a receipt."

THE CHRONICLE OF PHILANTHROPY JOSEPH A. BROWN

ZiGGY®

philanthropy illustrated
Committees

VIETOR'S **FUNNY BUSINESS**

"You didn't raise much money,
but you've been a fun committee."

WHOEVER THINKS TALK IS CHEAP HASN'T LISTENED TO OUR FINANCE COMMITTEE DREAMING UP NEXT YEAR'S BUDGET!

philanthropy illustrated

Communication

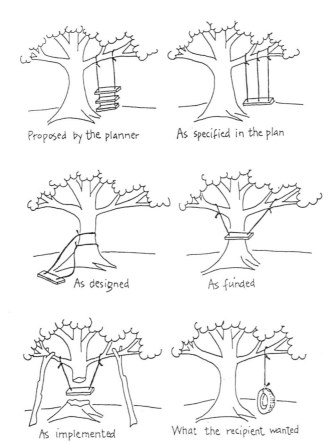

Proposed by the planner

As specified in the plan

As designed

As funded

As implemented

What the recipient wanted

philanthropy illustrated
Contributions

"What's the cause? Can't you just give?
Must there always be a cause?"

"SHIPWRECKED OR NOT I NEVER MISS SENDING OUT MY ANNUAL CONTRIBUTIONS!"

Joseph A. Brown

A little girl went to see the president of the bank explainingz that her girls' club was raising money, and would he please contribute.

The banker laid a dollar and a dime on the desk and said, "Take whichever you want."

The little girl picked up the dime and said, "My mother always taught me to take the smallest piece." However, picking up the dollar bill also, she added, "But so I won't lose this dime, I'll take this piece of paper to wrap it up in."

The businessman handed his young visitor a dollar, for which he received an "Associate Membership" card in the local boys' club.

"Now that I am a member," the businessman said, "just what are my rights and privileges?"

After thinking the matter over carefully the boy replied, "Well, it gives you the right to contribute next year."

"I say the next time we decide to help save an endangered species, we just give a cash donation."

THE CHRONICLE OF PHILANTHROPY

JOSEPH A. BROWN

"What do you mean you gave at the office?
This IS the office!"

philanthropy illustrated

A Development Officer Evaluation

Guide to Development Officer Performance Evaluation

Performance Factors	Far Exceeds Job Requirements	Exceeds Job Requirements	Meets Job Requirements	Needs Some Improvement	Does Not Meet Minimum Requirements
		Degrees of Performance			
Quality	Leaps tall buildings in a single bound	Must take running start to leap over tall buildings	Can leap over short buildings only	Crashes into buildings when attempting to jump over them	Cannot recognize buildings at all
Timelines	Is faster than a speeding bullet	Is as fast as a speeding bullet	Not quite as fast as a speeding bullet	Would you believe a slow bullet?	Wounds self with bullets when attempting to shoot
Initiative	Is stronger than a locomotive	Is stronger than a bull elephant	Is stronger than a bull	Shoots the bull	Smells like a bull
Adaptability	Walks on water	Walks on water in emergencies	Washes with water	Drinks water	Passes water in emergencies
Communication	Talks with God	Talks with angels	Talks to himself	Argues with himself	Loses most arguments

philanthropy illustrated

Foundations

"IT'S SETTLED THEN. THE FOUNDATION'S PRIORITIES FOR 1995 WILL BE THE ENVIRONMENT, WOMEN'S ISSUES, AND AGREEING TO A SCHEDULE ON THE TIME SHARING CONDO IN ASPEN."

Mark Litzler

"*. . . but this is easier than setting up a foundation!*"

THE CHRONICLE OF PHILANTHROPY

JOSEPH A. BROWN

PARTIAL FUNDING
PROVIDED BY THE
ROCKEFELLER
FOUNDATION

Carole Cable

" I'M ESTABLISHING MY OWN FOUNDATION."

Mark Litzler

philanthropy illustrated
Fund Raising

"No, I don't think we could call the building-fund
drive a success."

Top Ten Reasons for Becoming a Fund Raiser

#10—We were inspired by a Sally Struthers infomercial.

#9—For the glamour and the profit sharing plan.

#8—We take rejection well.

#7—What else can a liberal arts graduate do?

#6—We *need* to change jobs every 1.7 years.

#5—I thought if I raised money in the capital campaign,
they'd name the building after me.

#4—We can use the word "athon" after almost any verb.

#3—We want everyone to have an opportunity to become
our boss.

#2—Dinner at the Waldorf twice a week.

#1—My parole officer said that would qualify as
community service.

Recorded at Fund Raising Day in New York
by Steven M. Bernstein

"I think we should organize a campaign
to raise money for air conditioning."

"A bake sale may be tried and true, Isabel,

but we're trying to raise $5-million here."

Christopher Burke

WINTHROP

MY DAD WAS APPOINTED CHAIRMAN OF HIS CLUB'S FUND-RAISING COMMITTEE.

HE'S PRETTY MAD ABOUT IT. HE SAYS THAT IF HE HADN'T MISSED THAT MEETING...

HE WOULDN'T HAVE BEEN APPOINTED CHAIRMAN.

WINTHROP reprinted by permission of Newspaper Enterprise Association, Inc.

GRANTLAND®

TO ALL OF YOU WHO HAVE COME TO OUR GALA BENEFIT,

WELCOME... AND THANK YOU –

–FOR SUPPORTING US AND FOR BEING HERE TONIGHT. BUT MOST OF ALL,

THANK YOU FOR BEING RICH.

Copyright, Grantland Enterprises, Inc.; 460 Bloomfield Ave., Montclair, NJ 07042

"Jon Olson, hospital fund raiser, here... I'd like a hand with my administrator, a little of your input regarding the chairman of our foundation, some of your help in finishing our case statement...and some major assistance with my back swing."

"At one point, our opera company's fund-raising and promotions person had me considering an onstage spaghetti-eating contest with Pavarotti."

THE CHRONICLE OF PHILANTHROPY   KENNETH KAHN

Important Questions for the Fund Raising Profession

Fund raisers are nothing if not inquisitive. Yet, curiously, there are serious unresolved issues that continue to impede our growth as a profession. I submit for your consideration the following perplexing questions for these confusing times. The collective dignity of the fund raising profession may rest with the resolution of these timely and important issues.

- Is fund raising one word or two?

- If a donor makes a pledge in the woods, and nobody hears it, is a gift really made?

- What is the difference between a nonprofit organization and a not-for-profit organization?

- Why don't fund raisers ever get credit for restricted and planned gifts?

- What percentage of feasibility studies actually recommend against proceeding with a campaign?

- Can fund raisers write anything over their own signature?

- Why does the chairperson of the board always receive duplicate copies of our last direct mail appeal?

- Why is the grants process different in each foundation?

- Are LYBNTY's contagious? Can they be treated? Does Penicillin help?

- Does public relations support fund raising or vise versa?

- Why do PR people hang their plaque in their office that reads "Illigitatum non-carborundum"?

- Why do board members bring us articles from *The New York Times* about $50 million grants to other organizations?

- Why are we never the other organization?

- When is a direct mail test over?

- How often should we mail to our donors? Is twice enough, is 18 too many? What's a fund raiser to do?

- Should there be uniform standards for concepts like "major donors" and "lapsed givers?"

- Did the computer know it was June 29 when it crashed?

- What is the appropriate number of jobs a fund raiser should have in a given six-month period?

- When responding to a blind classified ad, how many fund raisers have actually applied for their own positions?

- If fund raisers cease all activities, would the same amount of money be raised anyway?

- What were the real career objectives of most fund raisers?

- Why do nominating committees ask fund raisers to suggest new board members and then ignore these suggestions?

- Should there be legislation that prohibits fund raising consultants from calling their firms "John Smith and Associates" if there are no associates?

- If there were an annual convention for all of these "Associates," would anyone be there?

- When do those fund raisers who speak at every fund raising convention actually raise any funds?

- Are all fund raisers consultants? Are all consultants between jobs?

- How many alumni/ae can squeeze into a telephone booth: Into a $100 gift?

- What's the real reasons fund raisers won't work for a percentage of funds raised?

- How may fund raisers does it take to change a light bulb?*

*Note: We'll let you know when the consultants have completed the feasibility study.

by Stephen M. Bernstein

O. K., GOD . . .
NOW WHAT ABOUT
FUNDING THIS PROJECT?

Artist could not be located.

LITZLER

"YOUR LEAD GIFT FOR THE CAMPAIGN IS CRITICAL.
IT HAS GOT TO SET THE PACE. IT HAS GOT TO
EXCITE THE COMMITTEE. IT HAS GOT TO KICK-
OFF THE VOLUNTEERS. IT HAS GOT TO BE
MORE THAN $200."

Mark Litzler

MOMMA MELL LAZARUS

By permission of Mell Lazarus and Creators Syndicate.

Reprinted with permission of Jerold Panas, Linzy & Partners.

GRANTLAND®

Put not your trust in money, put your money in trust.

—*Oliver Wendell Holmes*

CHAMBER CHUCKLES

**"Hey! This just might be the break
we've been looking for!"**

When I was young I thought that money was the
most important thing in life; now that I am old, I know
that it is.

—Oscar Wilde

"My son, you say you seek contentment, peace-of-mind, and serenity. Tell me, why are you in hospital fund raising?"

BERRY'S WORLD

© 1971 by NEA, Inc.

"I was feeling sorry for myself, and in came a man who was less fortunate than I. The poor fellow was on a fund-raising committee for some worthy cause or other."

A rich man told me recently that a liberal is a man who tells other people what to do with their money.

"I'M SURE YOUR COUSIN HERE DOES HAVE AN UNCANNY TALENT FOR RAISING FAST CASH. I WAS THINKING MORE ALONG THE LINES OF A BAKE SALE."

Lila Bauman

LITZLER

"THIS SEEMS AS GOOD A TIME AS ANY TO BRING UP THE LIKELIHOOD OF YOUR FUNDING OUR LECTURE SERIES ON IMAGES OF SALVATION AND DAMNATION."

Mark Litzler

"I USED TO BE IN PROFESSIONAL INSTITUTIONAL FUND-RAISING."

Harley L. Schwadron

I do everything for a reason. Most of the time the reason is money.

—*Suzy Parker*

"I THINK I'VE FOUND THE GUY TO LEAD OUR NEXT FUND-RAISING DRIVE."

philanthropy illustrated
Grants

"The best grants lie that-a-ways, Ma'am."

Christopher Burke

"I remain, through the current academic year, grantfully yours, ..."

Carole Cable

LITZLER

"YOU KNOW I THINK WE HAD THE
GRANT APPROVED RIGHT UP TO WHEN
SHE COUNTED ALL THE ZEROS ON
THE FUNDING AMOUNT."

Mark Litzler

"CONGRATULATIONS. YOU'RE OUR 15TH CALLER. THE GRANT IS YOURS."

Christopher Burke

"IN RETROSPECT I HAVE TO SAY SOME OF THE INDIRECT EXPENSES WERE NOT RELATED PER SE TO THE GRANT."

Mark Litzler

ESPRESSO
CAPPUCCINO

Cable

"What you need is a grant to give you some free time to write a really first-rate proposal."

Carole Cable

PERSONAL: GRANT WRITER SEEKS PRIVATE FOUNDATION FOR ROMANTIC CORRESPONDENCE, COURTSHIP, AND POSSIBLE LONG TERM RELATIONSHIP...

LITZLER

Mark Litzler

LITZLER

"THE TRUSTEES REFERRED YOUR PROPOSAL
TO THEIR 'WHEN PIGS FLY' SUB COMMITTEE."

Mark Litzler

philanthropy illustrated
Holiday Giving

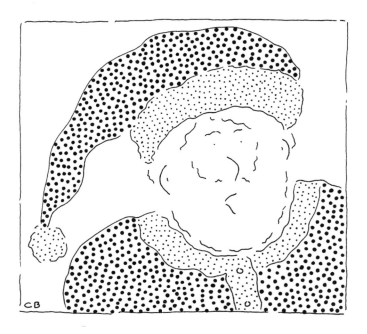

*"Ho, Ho, Ho, 'tis the
season to bequeath and
bestow."*

Christopher Burke

Just in Time for Christmas: A Generic Fund Raising Letter

by Steven M. Bernstein

'Tis the season for direct mail and I thought fund raisers could benefit from a "generic" appeal which can be tailored to each cause. The following is my holiday gift to the profession:

Dear (Friend, Neighbor, Donor, Bob):

Please give so little Suzie can (walk, talk, sing, fly) again.

We need your (gift, pledge, commitment, sworn affidavit) even more this year.

Last year you supported our (capital, annual, emergency) campaign. Won't you now consider (giving, renewing, upgrading) this year?

As a token of our appreciation we will be happy to send you a (premium, reward, bribe, chachka).

If you don't have the money now, we would be happy to accept your (pledge, promise, bank card) over the next few years.

Please use the enclosed (postage-paid, pre-stamped, free) envelope.

Sincerely,

(chairman, president, pretentious celebrity, fictitious person)

"... AND I WANT MORE BOARD MEMBERS TO MAKE PERSONAL CONTRIBUTIONS... AND I WANT A MAJOR BEQUEST TO COME IN... AND I WANT BETTER BOARD MEETING ATTENDANCE..."

Mark Litzler

philanthropy illustrated
The I.R.S.

"Now this $1-million contribution I made, was it
a sincere gesture or just for tax purposes?"

THE CHRONICLE OF PHILANTHROPY

JOSEPH A. BROWN

"What's this we hear about you laying up treasures in heaven?"

"I've got a little job for you, Kretchmer. I want you to infiltrate the I.R.S. and sow the seeds of compassion."

"But I thought once the I.R.S. applied a penalty, that was the end of it."

Drawing by Stevenson; © 1979 The New Yorker Magazine, Inc.

"I UNDERSTAND YOU MAY HAVE SOME PULL WITH THE I.R.S.

Harley L. Schwadron

Death and taxes may always be with us, but death at least doesn't get any worse.

"This donation is extremely generous, especially since the IRS has ruled that gifts to our organization are no longer tax-deductible."

JOSEPH A. BROWN

"LET ME GET THIS STRAIGHT..... YOU NEGLECTED TO DEDUCT A SIXTY-NINE THOUSAND DOLLAR BUSINESS LOSS, BUT YOU'RE CLAIMING A TWO DOLLAR DONATION OF USED UNDERWEAR?"

"*Welcome aboard. You are now exempt
from federal, state, and local taxes.*"

Drawing by Bernard Schoenbaum; © 1990 The New Yorker Magazine, Inc.

THERE IS ONE CONSOLATION TO THE POOR GETTING THEIR REWARD IN HEAVEN ... AT LEAST THEY WON'T HAVE TO PAY TAXES ON IT!

Artist could not be located.

Need is defined as my wanting something you have. Greed is defined as my wanting to keep it. And, compassion is when the government wants to handle the transaction.

In light of the new I.R.S. regulation, NSFRE member, Steven Bernstein offers this creative suggestion for your organization's donor acknowledgment letter.

Mr. John Doe
123 Main Street
Anywhere, NY 10000

Thank you so very much for your generous gift of $100, dated February 26, 1996.

For your records, no goods or services were furnished by us in connection with the above mentioned gift; no member of our staff will benefit, materially or otherwise, as a result of your gift; no intrinsic value, other than the actual face value, has been applied to your gift; and no significant pleasure was taken by us in the receipt of your gift.

This acknowledgment letter, having been prepared on recycled paper by an overworked and underpaid secretary, does not in itself constitute a good or service in exchange for your gift. In fact, given the small size of your gift, there is every possibility that processing the correspondence associated with your gift exceeds its cash value.

Sincerely,

Steven M. Bernstein
Executive Director

"HE HAS SOME QUESTIONS ABOUT YOUR TRUST FUND SET UP."

"Look, Mr. Claus, as your tax consultant I'm advising you to go with a foundation this year. No more freelancing!"

THE CHRONICLE OF PHILANTHROPY

JOSEPH A. BROWN

philanthropy illustrated
Major Donors

LITZLER

"YOU OUGHT TO KNOW ABOUT OUR NEW GIFT CLUB FOR LONG-SHOT MAJOR DONORS... IT'S CALLED THE DIVINE INTERVENTION SOCIETY."

Mark Litzler

"Ms. Jones, I seem to be suffering from an image problem. Please send out a large anonymous donation to a charitable organization, then notify the newspapers!"

JOSEPH A. BROWN

"OUR DONOR TRACKING SERVICE IDENTIFIED ME AS THE PERSON LEAST LIKELY TO MAKE A MAJOR GIFT."

Carole Cable

"Ms. Johnson, I've decided to make a large donation to my favorite charity. Please find out which one that is, and get back to me!"

THE CHRONICLE OF PHILANTHROPY

JOSEPH BROWN

"When I gave half a million dollars to the church, I didn't count on being blessed with such good health that I would outlive my assets."

THE CHRONICLE OF PHILANTHROPY

MARK LITZLER

WHEN THEY SAID "_NON_-DONOR'S WALL
I THOUGHT THEY WERE KIDDING!

Lila Bauman

" NOW THAT WE'VE ENDOWED YOUR $1 MILLION CHAIR IN ETHICS, I'D LIKE YOU TO TAKE A SECOND LOOK AT JUNIOR'S ENTRANCE EXAM AND INTERVIEW. "

Mark Litzler

philanthropy illustrated
Miscellaneous

EXECUTIVE SUITE reprinted by permission of Newspaper Enterprise Association, Inc.

William Wells & Jack Lindstrom

The drive-in bank was established so that the real owner of a car could get to see it once in a while.

Always borrow from a pessimist—he never expects it back.

Before you borrow money from a friend, decide which you need more.

I don't make jokes. I just watch the government and report the facts.

—*Will Rogers*

I got the bill for my surgery. Now I know why those doctors were wearing masks.

"It may be a vast untapped market, David, but who's going to advertise in the 'Welfare Recipient Weekly'?"

Nick Hobart

Kenneth Kahn

Harley L. Schwadron

"ALL THIS E-MAIL... I MISS SCHMOOZING."

Mark Litzler

Credit is a system whereby a person who can't pay gets another person who can't pay to guarantee that he can pay.

—*Charles Dickens*

The art of government consists in taking as much as possible from one class of citizens to give to another.

—*Voltaire*

Laugh and the world laughs with you, snore and you sleep alone.

Humor is civilization's escape valve.

Artist could not be located.

The saving grace of America lies in the fact that the overwhelming majority of Americans possess a sense of humor.

—*Franklin D. Roosevelt*

"Actually, Mr. Beasley, we were hoping for a more concrete pledge."

Nick Hobart

Nick Hobart

philanthropy illustrated

Nonprofits

"I'M SORRY, SIR, WE'RE A
NON-PROPHET ORGANIZATION."

Lila Bauman

"HE'S ONE IN A MILLION, HE MADE A PROFIT, HEADING UP A NON PROFIT MAKING ORGANIZATION."

Bob Schochet

"A table for two. Would you prefer to be seated in profit or in non-profit?"

Christopher Burke

"Oh dear, my dear, I'm afraid the tall, dark stranger works at a non-profit."

Christopher Burke

"NO, I DISTINCTLY SAID TO BRING IN A PROFIT."

Bob Schochet

"We who are gathered here today contributed, in lieu of gifts, to the following non-profit organizations."

Carole Cable

philanthropy illustrated
Philanthropy

"WELL, I SUPPOSE YOU COULD SAY I'M SORT OF A PHILANTHROPIST..."

B.C.
by johnny hart

By permission of Johnny Hart and Creators Syndicate, Inc.

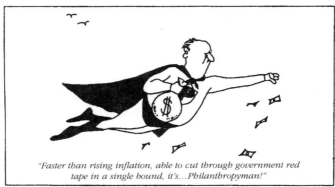

"Faster than rising inflation, able to cut through government red tape in a single bound, it's...Philanthropyman!"

THE CHRONICLE OF PHILANTHROPY   JOSEPH A. BROWN

SNAFU® by Bruce Beattie

"I want to give away enough money to be considered a philanthropist...and not a penny more!"

"Philanderer, philanthropist - whatever they called it, it was a nice award."

Contributions Magazine

" TODAY WE'RE INTERVIEWING A LONG-TIME, WELL KNOWN PHILANTHROPIST... "

philanthropy illustrated
Phonathons

" ... SORRY. WE GAVE IN THE CAR. "

Mark Litzler

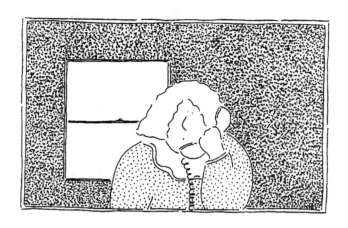

"Yes, Mrs. Muldoon. We have unfortunately, at this point in time, completely used up your generous thirty dollar contribution of last year."

Christopher Burke

"WITH 'CALLER I.D.' I CAN SEE IF IT'S MY SON, DAUGHTER, CHURCH, OR PLANNED GIVING OFFICER CALLING FOR MONEY."

Mark Litzler

"*Another record-breaking night. They ate more than they raised in donations*"

philanthropy illustrated
Proposals

LITZLER

"I'M AT THAT AWKWARD POINT IN THE PROPO-
SAL WHERE I HAVE TO ASK FOR SOMETHING."

Mark Litzler

FUNNY BUSINESS

Does this mean my proposal is turned down?"

"AS WE CONSIDER THE PROPOSALS, LET'S NOT FORGET WHO INCLUDED A GALLON OF ROCKY ROAD AS 'ATTACHMENT B'."

Mark Litzler

philanthropy illustrated
Religious

THE
BENEVOLENT
SHALL
INHERIT
THE EARTH

SCHOCHET

Bob Schochet

"Are we glad to hear that you don't know where you'll get the money you need. For a minute there we were afraid you wanted to get it from us."

"My husband will be missing four Sundays. Last Sunday he put a five-dollar bill in the collection plate thinking it was a one-dollar bill."

A clergyman received a phone call from the local income-tax man inquiring about a $535 contribution listed as having been paid his church by a parishioner. "Did he make this donation?" the tax man asked. The clergyman hesitated, then replied: "No—but he will, he will."

"He says it encourages people to add a fifteen percent gratuity to their offerings."

Nick Hobart

A commercial flight was experiencing considerable turbulence. One first-time traveler began praying. "Lord, " he said, "I'm a rich man. If you just let this plane land safely, I'll give you half of everything I own."

The plane landed and this gentleman was the first one off. In the terminal, a preacher tapped him on the shoulder, "Sir," he said, "I was on that plane with you, and I heard your prayer. Well, I'm a man of the cloth, and I'm here to collect."

"I made the Lord a better offer," the rich man said. "I told him if he ever catches me on a plane again, he can have it all!"

—*Contributed to* Readers Digest *March 1986 by Gene Perret*

If you had $10,000 would you give it to the Lord? Oh yes, I surely would.

If you had $500 would you give it to the Lord? I sure would.

If you had $10 would you give it to the Lord? Now wait a minute, I've got ten dollars!"

"No sir, it wasn't your sermon.
He accidentally put his hundred dollar bill
in the collection plate!"

A young boy sent a letter to the post office, addressed to God. A postal employee, not knowing exactly what to do with it, gave it to the local rotary club. It read: "Dear God, my name is Jimmy. I am six years old. My father is dead and my mother is having a hard time raising me and my sister. Would you please send us $500?"

The Rotarians were touched and decided to pitch in a few dollars each and send whatever they collected to the family. They were able to raise $300. A couple weeks later, a second letter from Jimmy was turned over to them.

The boy thanked God but ended with this request: "Next time, would you please deliver the money directly to our home? If you send it to the Rotary Club, they deduct $200."

—*Peter E. Stolz, Rotarian; Menomonee Falls, WI.*

Episcopal Church Archives.

"Sorry — there's a $3 cover charge now."

Nick Hobart

MY SERMON "THE BEST THINGS IN LIFE ARE FREE" MUST HAVE BEEN REALLY CONVINCING. NO ONE PUT A THING IN THE COLLECTION PLATE!

Artist could not be located.

philanthropy illustrated
Social Issues

"I like your style, Charlie — you think big."

Nick Hobart

Harley L. Schwadron

"*Luckily, the paper published a special 30-page section on homelessness today.*"

NICK HOBART

" WE'VE BEEN DESIGNATED A POVERTY AREA "

Harley L. Schwadron

"Glad to help narrow the gap between rich and poor."

Nick Hobart

"Wow, Jake, I hope you carry liability insurance."

Nick Hobart

Nick Hobart

philanthropy illustrated
Volunteers

"Hello, J.G.? I've found a volunteer who's willing to head up the fund drive!"

"Excuse me. I'd like to volunteer to be a grant recipient at your foundation."

Christopher Burke

HEY, COULDN'T SOME OF YOU VOLUNTEER TO STAY AND HELP CLEAN UP?

Artist could not be located.

philanthropy illustrated
Wealth

*"You wish we were rich? Sweetheart, why didn't you
tell me that thirty years ago?"*

Advertising may be described as the science of arresting human intelligence long enough to get money from it.

There are more things in life to worry about than just money—like how to get a hold of it, for example.

Money isn't everything. In fact, it usually isn't even enough.

"Sixteen requests for contributions in one day! My, doesn't that make you feel wealthy?"

*"These dreams of yours wherein you find great tubs of money,
Mr. Croy—can you describe the spot a little more exactly?"*

It is better to give than to lend, and it costs about the same.

If you want to see a short summer, borrow some money due in the fall.

Even the wisest among men welcome people who bring money more than those who take it away.

—*G. C. Lichtenberg*

Money speaks a language all nations understand.

—*Aphra Behn*

In God we trust; all others must pay cash.

—*American saying*

When it is a question of money, everybody is the same religion. —*Voltaire*

Money will hide many faults. —*Miguel de Cervantes*

Wealth is power usurped by the few, to compel the many to labor for their benefit. —*P.B. Shelley*

A wealthy man will always have followers. —*African Proverb*

MONEY, n: A blessing that is of no advantage to us excepting when we part with it. —*Ambrose Bierce*

It saves a lot of trouble if, instead of having to earn money and save it, you can just go and borrow it. —*Winston Churchill*

Nothing is more admirable than the fortitude with which millionaires tolerate the disadvantages of their wealth. —*Rex Stout*

Money is a soap that removes the worst stains. —*Jewish Proverb*

The rich man and his daughter are soon parted. —*Frank McKinney Hubbard*

Money is the best bait to fish for man with. —*Thomas Fuller*

Remember, you can't take it with you, and if you could, it would probably melt. —*Frank A. Logan*

FRANK & ERNEST® by Bob Thaves

YES, THE OPERATION MADE A NEW MAN OUT OF ME --- THE OLD ONE HAD SOME MONEY IN THE BANK.

NURSE

THAVES 2-20

© 1989 by NEA, Inc.

*"I've learned to live without a lot of things, Herb,
but money isn't one of them."*

Bibliography

Cartoonists and Syndicates

Lila Bauman, Cartoonist
350 E. 30th St., Apt. 2-F
New York, NY 10016
212-545-8756
e-mail: ldb202@is5.nyu.edu

Joseph A. Brown, Cartoonist
1220 Nassau Street
Kalamazoo, MI 49001
616-342-4637

Christopher Burke, Cartoonist
209 Lincoln Place, Apt. 7-D
Brooklyn, NY 11217
718-636-8739

(Ford Button cartoon)
Joyce Button
3398 Chili Ave.
Rochester, NY 14624
716-889-3045

Carole Cable, Cartoonist
902 Live Oak Ridge
Austin, TX 78746
512-495-4382
e-mail:
carole.cable@mail.utexas.edu

Dave Carpenter, Cartoonist
Box 520
Emmetsburg, IA 50536
712-852-3725

Cartoons by Johns
Box 1300
Pebble Beach, CA 93953
408-649-0303

Tom Cheney, Cartoonist
P.O. Box 73
Watertown, NY 13601

Contributions Magazine
P.O. Box 336
Medfield, MA 02052-0336
617-964-2688

(Momma, B.C., & The Wizard
of ID cartoons)
Creator's Syndicate
5777 W. Century Blvd.
Suite 700
Los Angeles, CA 90045
310-337-7003
fax: 310-337-7625

Episcopal Church Archives
P.O. Box 2247
Austin, TX 78768
800-525-9329

Philip Frank, Cartoonist
500 Turney Street
Sausalito, CA 94965
415-332-1297

Grantland Enterprises Inc.
Grant Brownrigg, Cartoonist
460 Bloomfield Ave., Suite 307
Montclair, NJ 07042
201-509-7688
fax 201-509-9588

Nick Hobart, Cartoonist
5632 Indiana Ave.
New Port Richey, FL 34652
813-849-2972

Ken Kahn, Cartoonist
6028 Winifred Drive
Ft. Worth, TX 76133
817-870-2564

(Beetle Bailey, Hagar the
Horrible, Jim Borgman
cartoons)
King Features Syndicate
235 E. 45th Street
New York, NY 10017
212-455-4000
fax: 212-682-9763

Mark Litzler, Cartoonist
10130 Linden
Overland Park, KS 66207
816-556-3159
e-mail: Mlitzler@cctr.umkc.edu

(Chamber Chuckles cartoon)
Gene Machamer, Cartoonist
P.O. Box 747
Mechanicsburg, PA 17055

Dale McFeatters, Cartoonist
1461 Navaho Dr.
Pittsburgh, PA 15228
412-561-5382

Joe McKeever, Cartoonist
P.O. Box 1357
Kenner, LA 70063-1357
504-466-5381

(Franscino, Weber, Price,
Schoenbaum, Stevenson,
Miller & Wilson cartoons)
The New Yorker Magazine,
Inc.
Permissions Dept.
20 West 43rd St.
New York, NY 10036-7441
212-840-3800
fax: 212-536-5735

Jerold Panas, Linzy &
Partners
500 N. Michigan
Chicago, IL 60611
312-222-1212

Bob Schochet, Cartoonist
Sunset Road
Highland Mills, NY 10930
914-928-2885

Bernard Schoenbaum,
Cartoonist
27 Angle Lane
Hicksville, NY 11801
516-935-0125

Harley L. Schwadron,
Cartoonist
P.O. Box 1347
Ann Arbor, MI 48106
313-426-8433

(Frank & Ernest cartoon)
Bob Thaves, Cartoonist
P.O. Box 67
Manhattan Beach, CA 90266
310-412-8622

(Shoe cartoon)
Tribune Media Services
435 N. Michigan Ave.
Suite 1500
Chicago, IL 60611
800-245-6536; 312-222-
4382 fax: 312-222-2581

(Peanuts, Berry's World, Exec.
Suite, SNAFU & Winthrop
cartoons)
United Features Syndicate &
Newspaper Enterprise
Association, Inc.
c/o United Media
200 Madison Ave.
New York, NY 10016
212-293-8500
fax: 212-293-8619

(Ziggy & Jules Feiffer
cartoons)
Universal Press Syndicate
Permissions Dept.
4900 Main Street
Kansas City, MO 64112
816-932-6600

(*Vietor's* Funny Business
cartoon)
USA Today Library Research
Services
Reprint & Permissions Dept.
1000 Wilson Blvd.
Arlington, VA 22229
703-276-3400
fax: 703-247-3139

Articles by Steven M.
Bernstein may be reprinted,
with proper credit given.

(Unknown Artists)
*Every effort was made to
locate the cartoonists who's
works are used in this book.
However, a few could not be
located. These cartoons may
be reprinted with* Accent on
Humor III *listed as the source.
If a cartoonist is known to
you, please notify
Philanthropic Services so we
can give proper credit for
their work.*

The majority of the copy in
Accent on Humor III *was
collected from readers of the
first two editions of the book.
Also, a few quips came from:*
Humorous Quotes. *Great
Quotations, Inc., Lombard, IL:
1984, and* Money Talks. *Peter
Pauper Press, Inc., White
Plains, NY; 1988.*

Acknowledgments

Special thanks to the Milton Murray Foundation for Philanthropy for partially sponsoring the publishing of this third edition of *Accent on Humor*.

Cartoon Donations: Lila Bauman
                       Episcopal Church Archives
                       Gene Machamer
                       Dale McFeatters
                       Joe McKeever
                       Jerold Panas, Linzy & Partners

Your favorite cartoon or humorous anecdote could appear in the next edition of *Accent on Humor.* Please submit humorous material to the address below.

Philanthropic Service for Institutions
Adventist World Headquarters
12501 Old Columbia Pike
Silver Spring, MD 20904-6600
phone: 301-680-6135, fax: 301-680-6137

* Any material in this book containing religious overtones is in no way making a statement of belief or doctrine of the publisher.